WHILE AND WHY YOU FAIL

It is important to know why you failed and what to do while you fail

Edna Sears

TABLE OF CONTENT

INTRODUCTION

Failure is painful and difficult, but it is a necessary part of success. The way you respond to failure will determine whether you will succeed.

Always being unsuccessful is discouraging and upsetting. You can't always control when or if tough things will happen to you, but you can greatly influence how you respond to them. Failure causes your mind to deceive you into believing falsehoods. Failures will paralyze you, demotivate you, and reduce your chances of success in the future unless you learn to respond to them in psychologically adaptive methods

The most crucial psychological action following a setback is to comprehend its effects, including how it impacts your attitudes, sentiments, and actions.

Those who missed the mark thought it was higher and further away than those who made it. In other words, when you fail, your impression of your objectives is automatically distorted, making them seem more out of reach. The keyword here is "distort" because your objectives remain the same as they were prior to your failure, all that has changed is the way you perceive them. These new perceptions are yours to reject, and you should. In actuality, failure does not just alter your vision of your goals, it also alters how you perceive yourself. Failure also distorts your judgments of your actual talents by making you feel less capable of the work, which further distances your goals from your grasp. After failing, you're more inclined to make a mistaken assessment of your abilities and perceive them as being much weaker than they actually are. Understanding this is important, because doing otherwise will cause you to undervalue your skills.

Failure leaves you feeling helpless.

Helplessness is among the emotions that people experience after failing the most frequently and intensely. Failure leaves a psychological scar. Your mind reacts to this injury by attempting to persuade you to give up in order to prevent further injury, and the only way it knows how to do this is by making you feel helpless. Your mind may prevent future failures by making you feel as though there is nothing you can do to succeed, but you will also be deprived of present accomplishments. For this reason, you shouldn't always pay attention to your feelings. However, there are other ways your mind might operate against you.

Instead of wallowing in your past mistakes, always remember to learn from each failure.

CHAPTER ONE

WHY PEOPLE FAILS IN LIFE

If you look closely at some of history's most successful individuals, you'll see that they all failed utterly. The majority of these individuals were widely viewed as tragic life failures. They performed a magic trick, turning defeat into victory. How did they succeed in doing this? They discovered the reasons why they failed, learned important lessons from them, and changed their perspective on failure. You must understand that achieving success does not require doing everything properly the first time. Instead, it is something you gradually learn to avoid doing.

Everyone makes errors. Unavoidable, this is something that must be done. However, we always have the choice to use these frequently trying situations as a springboard for future growth.

1. Lack of Networking Willpower:

You'll miss out on many opportunities if you don't take the time to build solid connections with people who can support and assist you. Sadly, a lot of individuals minimize the importance of socializing. Through our relationships, we can reach out to others and persuade them to side with us rather than against us. We can meet people who share our interests through networking and socializing.

Spending quality time with friends, making new friends, networking with others, and taking part in social activities like partying, playing games, going out, and other things are all part of having an active social life. A passive social life, on the other hand, denotes a lack of engagement in social activities. A person with a passive social life may prefer to observe rather than participate in social activities, and they may enjoy spending time alone, having a small group of close friends, occasionally going to social events, staying indoors, or having private conversations rather than engaging in group conversations. . However, it is useful to highlight that, while maintaining personal space and having a passive social life are good, having a steady social life is equally necessary and advantageous in many ways.

The following are some advantages of having a steady and moderately active social life:

- Making solid connections: Having a vibrant social life has several essential advantages. There are some things you can't reach until you have someone's contact information, and it's been said that your network determines your net worth. Due to the possibility that they will come in handy to save you tomorrow or present lucrative chances for you today, making solid connections is crucial. By interacting with others, talking to friends, making new acquaintances at social gatherings, networking with influential individuals. An active social life makes it easier to form connections.

- Obtaining Support: The engine that propels an automobile is support. Therefore, it is crucial to our desire for success and may be attained through an active social life because having excellent social relationships with others gives you trustworthy individuals in your life who you can rely on for support when things are tough.

2. Castigating others for your failure

Blaming others for your mistakes and problems will inevitably lead to failure. We're all dealing with problems at the same time that are leading us to go off course. If we stop using these problems and challenges as justifications, we will only make progress in life. Successful people don't let justifications stand in the way of completing their goals.

They understand that making excuses won't help them go forward. As a result, they refuse to provide a "feel-good justification," own up to errors, and start taking charge of the circumstance. There is always an explanation for being inactive. Stop allowing your fear of failure, embarrassment, or growth to keep you confined to your comfort zone.

3. Lack of Humility

Despite its unpopularity, humility is regarded by many successful people as a key contributor to success. Some others even think success demands it. Being humble has a few more advantages, It pushes you to constantly put others before yourself. You may assess your skills, flaws, and limitations genuinely when you are humble. However, it will help you realize that there are a lot of things you don't know. Many lack the essential ingredient of humility. Many failed or underperforming individuals lack humility. Because they've had some success in battle, they think they are experts in the art of war. This characteristic prevents advancement.

4. Lack of Self-Belief: Talent or intelligence aren't necessarily the defining characteristics that separate successful people from unsuccessful ones. The biggest difference is that successful people have self-confidence. They believe they can accomplish the goals they have for themselves. They have faith in their ability to solve the issues they are facing.

They are driven to take on projects that initially seem too big for them because they have a strong belief that they can work things out as they go. Successful people are aware that it is not a credit at all time. While failed people make excuses when things aren't going their way, successful people are determined to make things work for them. Therefore, it's essential to understand how important it is to have faith in what you're doing.

5. Too Much Haste:

There are many people who wish to accomplish great things. They set really challenging goals for themselves, but as soon as they see how high the mountain is, they become terrified. People quickly lose hope when they don't see results.

There is nothing improper about having lofty goals and aspirations. In some circumstances, soaring too high may put you at danger for a protracted and painful fall. However, it will encourage you to put in a lot of effort and strive for greatness in general. Setting grandiose goals without considering the everyday dedication, effort, and labor necessary to reach them is the real problem. This perspective holds that it is a serious issue if we strive for the stars without first thinking about how to get there. Humans naturally seek out instant gratification. Therefore, divide up your goals to avoid becoming discouraged too soon. Setting both significant and minor goals will help you stay motivated as you make your way to the top.

6. Fear of Failure

Our fear of failing terrifies us. It makes us reluctant to seize favorable opportunities. Because we are afraid of failing, we won't even try, even yet the biggest failure is not trying at all. There is no reason to be afraid of failing. Don't be afraid to try because you lack the courage to fail. It's crucial to understand that the fear of failing is a huge barrier to success. You will have made great progress after you defeat it. Only by moving forward step by step can anything be accomplished. If you make a few mistakes, it doesn't matter. It's crucial that you stand back up and continue moving forward.

Failure shouldn't be considered a penalty. Instead, use what you've learned from all of your failures to push harder to achieve your goals.

7. Lack of Adequate Planning

If you don't have a good plan, your chances of success are lower. Even if the plan is incorrect or things don't go as expected, it doesn't matter. The only thing that matters is the plan you have in place. This will help you focus all of your efforts in the same direction. If you don't have a clear plan, you'll probably find yourself going in circles and never accomplishing your goals.

The value of planning is supported by data showing that businesses with a strategy are less likely to fail. Make time-bound, detailed, measurable, and attainable strategies. Give a goal some thought before you start working toward it. Make plans for your next move and how you'll handle difficulties. Review your plans frequently and adjust as necessary.

8. A lack of persistence despite your talent and intelligence. You will certainly fail if you don't combine the two with perseverance. One of the biggest obstacles is a lack of persistence.

Perseverance is one of the biggest obstacles to success, because they place an excessive amount of dependence on their skills, a great number of exceptionally intelligent and successful people repeatedly fail. They are unwilling to try again and again until they have mastered what they are doing. Instead, they give up when things get difficult. If you think your failures are the result of a lack of perseverance, develop ways to prevent giving up too quickly. Perseverance is all about trying new things and making adjustments, even while it's true that persevering when you're stuck in a rut won't get you anywhere.

9. Lack of Self-Discipline:

To succeed, there is needs for self-control. Thus, keeping self-control is essential to success. If you lack self-control, you are more likely to give up quickly when problems arise. You are more likely to give in to transient pleasures when you lack discipline. If you lack discipline, you won't understand the benefit of making a sacrifice now for a reward tomorrow.

On the other hand, people who have principles will find it much easier to disregard diversions and distractions. Even if it means making short-term sacrifices, experiencing hardship, and avoiding distractions, self-control enables you to remain inspired and determined.

10. Refusing to heed counsel

Some people struggle because they refuse to take constructive criticism. Instead, they attempt to justify what they are doing for a variety of reasons. Even if their attempts fail, they continue to reject guidance. These people would rather be right than face themselves to criticism, at least from their own perspective. It is clear why this is the case. They want to avoid admitting their own shortcomings at all costs, thus they strive to avoid listening to criticism and other people's suggestions. Therefore, rather than learning how to do things correctly, they would prefer to persuade others that they are correct.

CHAPTER TWO

TIPS ON OVERCOMING FAILURE

1. Accepting emotions and feelings

Failure is associated with emotions and sentiments like depression, anxiety, tension, fury, and many more. Any person who experiences those feelings knows how uncomfortable they are and will try anything to get rid of them. The reality is that those sensations and emotions will actually motivate you to work harder and come up with new, better ideas so that you may do better the following time. Accept those feelings and emotions since suppressing them can result in negative coping techniques.

2. Failure does not spell the end of your life.

Failure does not define who you are or what your future holds, despite what many people believe. The reality is that failure is something that happens to you, not something that you are. We all experience failure in life, whether it be in our attempts to get a job, find love, or enroll in college, to name a few. Failures do not have to define you; doing so is entirely discretionary.

3. Be constructive and learn from mistakes.

One of the major obstacles and lessons you will face in life is how to learn from failure. Knowing what went wrong can make you mentally stronger than ever and enable you to set particular goals using amazing techniques. You experience failure and gain knowledge. You stumble and get back up. You recover, prepare to stand up, and accomplish your objectives.

4. Look for motivation

Get away from where you are right now and move on from your failure. Visit a different region of the world and meet a variety of people. When people are inspired, they frequently let the past go and focus on the future with renewed motivation. Nothing or anyone will be able to stop you from following your inspiration. Getting out of your own head and concentrating on knowledge from outside sources will help you see things from a fresh viewpoint.

5. Keep going

Make the mental effort to accept that giving up is never an option. Happy-making and time appreciation are important. Show yourself that you are capable of anything and prove to the doubters that they are mistaken with your deeds. Most importantly, those who persist and don't give up will succeed.

6. Show enthusiasm

On occasion, a lack of passion for something may be cited as a reason for failure. Otherwise, if you are motivated and willing to put a lot of effort into anything, you will feel enthusiastic about it. Be passionate about what you love, not what other people have forced upon you

7. Surround yourself with optimistic individuals

How you approach and handle failure depends greatly on your environment. Spend time with people that constantly inspire you. Being around upbeat individuals is the best approach to avoid adding to the worry and anxiety that are already on your mind.

8. Avoid solitary confinement

People frequently experience sadness, depression, irritability, anxiety, and tension when they fail. As a result, it's critical to feel at ease and surrounded by others. There are many different ways to surround yourself with others, including family, friends, supportive groups, and others. Remember that your mental and physical health

9. Your resilience while you struggle

When attempting to accomplish a new goal, challenges will inevitably arise, however, your success will be determined by how you respond to these challenges.

Weaknesses frequently bring up strong memories of some past trauma. Conversely, using your strengths often feels more like going about your daily business. Because of this, figuring out what you're really good at can be challenging.

CHAPTER THREE

Here are some methods to help you determine your strengths if you're unsure of what they are.

- Keep an eye out

Although the advice to "pay attention" may seem obvious, we frequently fail to notice our strengths because we are so focused on strengthening our deficiencies.

To identify your strengths, you may need to dig a little further. Unexpected praise for a task you completed quickly could be a warning flag.

- Remind yourself that failure is a necessary component of success.

You must constantly remind yourself that you will fail before you succeed in anything if you want to achieve success.

Keep this in the back of your mind whenever you encounter a challenge or fail totally. Additionally, keep in mind that the alternative is a lifetime if you are too terrified to face the inevitable failures that come along with achievement.

- Develop a positive outlook

Few people are aware of the mind's power. You must consciously choose to be upbeat rather than miserable when you fail.

It will be far more difficult to bounce back from failure if you decide to live a terrible life. But if you develop a positive outlook, you can bounce back from each loss without losing your motivation and drive.

Always keep in mind that having an optimistic outlook will result in better outcomes than having a negative outlook.

- Accept your faults instead than dwelling on them.

Your inclination will be to criticize yourself when you fail. However, ruminating on your setbacks and blaming yourself for your errors saps your strength. Instead you need to understand that mistakes will occur, and failure will happen. Once you come to terms with this, you can concentrate on defining your success.

- Look for growth opportunities.

Every setback and failure offers you a chance to develop. It's up to you to recognize the opportunity in your failure and turn it around. After failing, reexamine everything and look for new openings to bust through.

- Decide to be joyful.

Happiness is undoubtedly a decision; sadly, a lot of us choose to be unhappy. Sadness will be your default feeling when you fail, but try not to allow your failures to control how you feel.

Don't allow your success to determine how happy you are, either. If you make the decision to be joyful even in the worst circumstances, you will feel in control of your shortcomings.

- Utilize your errors to improve.

You will be able to develop the abilities necessary to master your art if you are at ease creating and accepting mistakes.

- Consider what to do next.

Once you have failed at anything, you need to figure out your next action. Being proactive is a wonderful quality to possess, and it is far preferable than moping around in misery and doing nothing to improve your circumstances. Instead of becoming stuck in failure, you can start moving toward success by making decisions about your subsequent course of action.

- Keep the mind that other people have also failed.

It frequently seems like everything is working against you when you fail. When you understand that failure does not only affect you, you can spur yourself on to stand up more quickly.

Failure is common, and everyone who has achieved success has experienced it numerous times. If they were able to bounce back from failure, you can too.

- Make a list of your past achievement

The sentiment of worthlessness is one that is intimately associated with failure. Make a list of all the times you succeeded in order to overcome this feeling. You can post this list wherever you can see it every day, like your mirror or the cover of your diary.Now, every time you have a lack of confidence, review that list to remind yourself of your accomplishments.

- Consider your previous defeat.

You should record your previous failures in the same way that you record your successes. You'll come to the realization that you've failed numerous times before and have always gotten back up after looking at this list of failures. What has changed this time around

Recognize your mistakes and utilize them as motivation instead of ignoring them.

When things are difficult, the resilient push through.

- Get motivated by your role models

We all have mentors, whether they be scicntists, businesspeople, educators, actors, musicians, politicians, humanitarians, or writers.These individuals can be a tremendous source of inspiration because they have experienced similar circumstances to our own. Therefore, read about them, listen to them, and watch them while you are experiencing failure. Discover how they overcome their challenges and use that information to improve your circumstances.

- Put your other objectives first.

When wc succeed at smaller jobs after failing at a larger activity, our confidence will increase. Therefore, concentrate your emphasis on achieving each of your smaller, more manageable goals. The modest actions you are taking will eventually bring you back to your major undertaking, which is easy to understand and motivating.

No matter how minor it may seem, a win is still a win.

- Imagine yourself succeeding

When we fail, sometimes it helps to close our eyes and visualize what success will look like. By picturing success, it becomes attainable for you rather than being something you can only dream about. Additionally, by maintaining your optimistic outlook, you provide yourself with the drive to keep moving forward on your path to achievement.

- Recall that choosing to continue failing is a decision.

Failure is inevitable, and it is up to you whether you continue to be in that situation. You must decide whether to keep trying in the face of setbacks or you will become stuck.

Failure is choosing to stay down after having the option to get back up, not falling down.

- Be in the company of edifying individuals.

If you spend too much time with toxic people, you will eventually adopt their pessimistic viewpoints. You need to surround yourself with upbeat people who can motivate you to rise again when failure has knocked you down.

Their brightness and positivity will inspire you and instill in you the confidence you need to achieve.

- Step backward

I am aware that I said you must move forward after a failure, but it can be highly beneficial to take a step back before doing so.

You can reassess your choices when you step back and gain a greater understanding of where you went wrong. Once you've found your position, you can start moving ahead with determination.

- Rearrange Yourself

Don't rush to start again after failing, you need to rearrange yourself, you need to re-strategies you move. You can regain control of your circumstances by making a strategy for the future based on the lessons you've learned from your errors. Additionally, knowing your destination and how to get there puts you in a better position to achieve.

CHAPTER FOUR

SUCCESS THROUGH FAILURE

The first time one tries something, they are excellent at it. Hard work, practice, and yes, even failure, are the keys to success. Young children must stumble and fall often when learning to walk in order to develop the balance necessary to stand up straight (and even then, they will still fall down). Children must attempt, practice, learn from their mistakes, and try again in order to master new abilities, whether they are learning to feed themselves, tie their shoes, or grasp long division.

Failure provides us with the chance to pick ourselves up, learn from our mistakes, and enhances our appreciation for success.

Failure makes it easier to find the secret of success.

Failure is therefore just a step in our journey rather than the end. It even permits us to question ourselves when it's essential, which advances us if it crosses our path and we are able to learn the necessary lessons from it.

Failure is a necessary precursor to success. Only a few are able to write it on their first attempt.

You ought to aim for failure. You won't succeed if you always play it safe. The suffering must be felt. The procedure is as follows

Move forward, fail, and learn.

Attempting to stand up after being struck down. You will fail your way to success no matter how many times you fail and no matter how many times people tell you that you can't. All you need is the determination to keep trying until you succeed. Always keep in mind that if you don't bury the seeds in the earth, a tree won't grow.

While you fail, these 3D are crucial.

- Devotion
- Discipline
- Decisive

Self-control experts spend less time pondering whether to engage in actions and behaviors that are inconsistent with their values or objectives. They are not preoccupied. They resist letting emotions or impulses guide their decisions. They are the designers of their own ideas and the steps they take to bring about a desired result. As a result, they are less susceptible to being sidetracked by temptation and exhibit higher levels of life satisfaction.

Practice diligence Every day

Self-control is an acquired behavior; it is not something we are born with. It also needs regular repetition and practice in order to be mastered, just like any other talent. It must become habitual

Self-discipline calls for effort and concentration, which can be exhausting. It can get harder and harder to maintain your willpower as time goes on. Therefore, work on developing your self-discipline by being diligent every day in a specific area related to a goal. This refers to the third stage again. You need a plan in order to exercise everyday diligence. Add it to your schedule and to-do list.

Start off by working out for ten or fifteen minutes each day if you're attempting to lose weight but don't exercise frequently (or at all). Start by going to bed 30 minutes earlier each night if you want to develop improved sleeping habits. Make a change in your grocery shopping routine and start meal prepping if you want to eat healthier. Take it slow. You can eventually add more objectives to your list as your thinking and behavior start to change.

CHAPTER FIVE

MOVE ON AND EXTEND FORGIVENESS TO YOURSELF

Many people struggle with self-forgiveness due to prior transgressions.

A common definition of forgiveness is the conscious choice to release sentiments of rage, wrath, and revenge toward someone who you feel has harmed you. Although you could be quite understanding of others, you might be much more harsh with yourself.

Everyone makes mistakes, but it's crucial for mental health and wellbeing to learn how to take responsibility for them, move past them, and forgive yourself.

Learn more about the advantages of self-forgiveness and investigate several techniques that could make it easier for you to do so.

How to Forgive Yourself Forgiving yourself does not entail absolving yourself of responsibility or represent weakness. Whether you forgive someone who has harmed you or yourself, doing so does not imply that you are endorsing the behavior.

- Accepting accountability

By forgiving someone, you are expressing your willingness to let go of the past and go on with your life without dwelling on things that have already happened and cannot be altered. Four important steps are suggested by one therapeutic approach to self-forgiveness as being beneficial.

The first step toward forgiving oneself is to face what one has done or what one has experienced. It's also the most challenging. It's time to acknowledge your actions if you have been blaming others, rationalizing, or otherwise trying to make your behavior appear acceptable.

- Demonstrate regret

You could feel a variety of unfavorable emotions after accepting responsibility, such as guilt and humiliation. It's totally acceptable, even beneficial, to feel guilty after doing something wrong. These regret and guilt sentiments might act as a catalyst for constructive change.

- Reverse the harm and rebuild trust

Even when you are forgiving yourself, making apologies is a crucial component of forgiveness. Forgiving yourself is more likely to persist when you feel like you've earned it, just like you might not forgive someone else unless they make it up to you in some way.

Finding a means to grow as a person and learn from the event is frequently necessary to forgive oneself.

You must comprehend your actions and your guilt in order to accomplish this. What actions can you do to stop the same actions from happening again in the future? Yes, you may have made a mistake, but you can learn from it so that you can make better decisions in the future.

If you refuse to forgive yourself you just pledge allegiance to failure

CONCLUSION

Success and failure are two related phenomena that define human existence. Failure should not be viewed as a tragedy because it is a necessary component of success. You will value success more once you have faced failure. It is incorrect to believe that only people who correctly answer the question the first time receive points. However, the reality is that failure is unavoidable and really promotes achievement. Even the top performers in their fields frequently experience failure. They've all learned to take their setbacks and turn them into opportunities for achievement.

So, don't be frightened to fail. When you learn from your mistakes and work to prevent them in the future, you will soon reach the pinnacle of success.

Failures happen frequently. When we encounter failure, we shouldn't be disappointed. Every setback we suffer in life will teach us priceless lessons, and as a result, we get better and better. This will enable us to improve in the future and ultimately be successful. We use the phrase "failures are stepping stones to success" because of this.

We have seen throughout the book that failure doesn't just happen—it almost always has a reason.

When you reflect on a failure, there are nearly always different things you could have done to prevent it or at the very least lessen the intensity of its effects.

We've also learned that there are easy yet effective actions you may take to almost completely eradicate long-term failure from your life. You may plan your life so that the good moments are prioritized and the inevitable negative moments are reduced to a minimum.

www.ingramcontent.com/pod-product-compliance
Lightning Source LLC
LaVergne TN
LVHW052100160826
845678LV00015B/3307

* 9 7 9 8 8 4 8 9 8 7 4 6 1 *